ULTIMATE

CHROMECAST

A Complete Beginners To Pro Instruction
Manual on How to Setup Your New
Chromecast in 3 minutes and Explore
Awesome Contents Online

BY

BANNER TOM
Copyrigh©2018

COPYRIGHT

Banner Tom

TABLE OF CONTENT

CHAPTER ONE

INTRODUCTION

Chromecast is an amazing digital device that is becoming popular, this device that is used to stream contents online with the aid of an internet connection directly on your Television.

This handy device is connected to a Television set which will grant you access to several services.

However, chromcast is powered by the aid of a USB cable, while you connect the chromecast into the HDMI port of your television set. All this cannot be achieve without the aid of a wi-fi connection.

CHAPTER TWO

HOW TO QUICKLY SETUP THE CHROMECAST

To set up your Chromecast, you'll require the Google Home application (some time ago the Google Cast application), accessible on iOS and Android. On the off chance that your Chromecast is a rummage or an eBay discover, you should need to pause for a minute to plant reset it before proceeding with so you're beginning with a fresh start.

Despite the fact that there are different ages of Chromecast and a pristine application, the general setup process hasn't changed much. Initially, unload your Chromecast, connect it to, and sit tight for it to control up. You can connect the USB link to the divider utilizing the included connector, or the USB port on the back of your TV (as long as it gives enough power—some more established TVs may not).

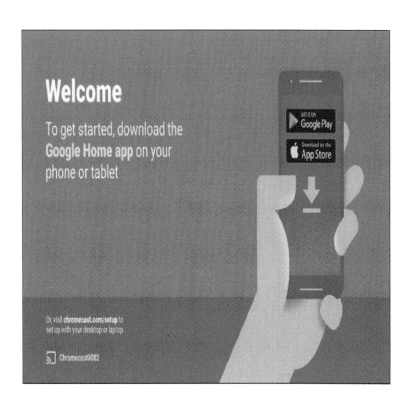

You'll know it's prepared for setup when see the on-screen provoke, demonstrated as follows. Note the haphazardly created identifier in the lower left corner. Our own is "Chromecast0082," however yours is likely unique.

With the setup provoke on your TV screen, now's an ideal opportunity to snatch your telephone or tablet and interface with the Chromecast to finish the setup procedure.

Contingent upon which age of Chromecast you have, the interfacing with bit is a slight extraordinary, so give careful consideration to the following area.

CHAPTER THREE

HOW TO SUCCESSFULLY CONNECT TO THE CHROMECAST

In spite of the fact that the setup procedure is to a great extent indistinguishable for all adaptations of the Chromecast, there is one major distinction between setting up an original Chromecast (which is a more drawn out dongle with a thumb-like shape) and the resulting ages (formed like circles), so listen intently to spare yourself a considerable measure of disappointment.

The second era Chromecast and the Chromecast Ultra both help Bluetooth. When you connect to another or industrial facility reset second era or Ultra model and begin the setup procedure with the Google Home application, you will be associated over Bluetooth promptly. In the event that it doesn't, ensure your telephone's Bluetooth is turned on.

In the event that you have an original Chromecast, nonetheless, you'll have to associate with the impermanent specially appointed Wi-Fi arrange it makes. Open your telephone or tablet's Wi-Fi settings and scan for a system with the special name we noted previously. On account of our demo display here, that is the "Chromecast0082.b" organize seen underneath.

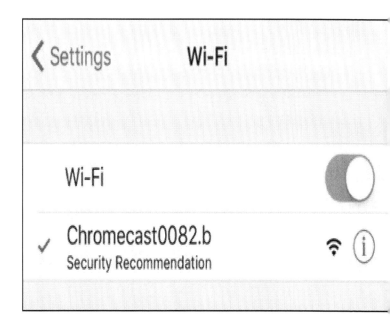

It's important that the specially appointed Wi-Fi arrange is likewise the fallback strategy for the more up to date ages as well. On the off chance that for any reason you get a mistake amid a Bluetooth-construct setup process in light of a more up to date display, you can simply open up the Wi-Fi menu on your telephone and utilize the old Wi-Fi technique.

CHAPTER FOUR

HOW TO QUICKLY CONFIGURE YOUR CHROMECAST

With your Chromecast associated with your telephone, it's a great opportunity to start up the Google Home application and complete the arrangement procedure. More often than not you'll be naturally incited to start the setup procedure right when you open the application, yet in the event that you aren't, don't stress. Basically tap the gadget symbol in the upper right corner, seen beneath.

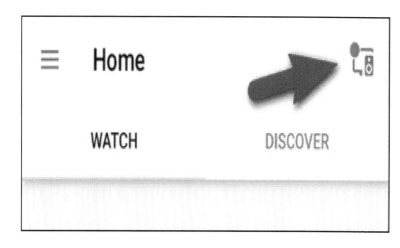

Gadgets that need setup are assembled at the highest point of the screen. Confirm the Chromecast identifier on your android device coordinates the identifier showed on your TV and tap "Set Up".

In the initial step of the setup procedure, the application will affirm the brief identifier assigned to the Chromecast. tap "Continue".

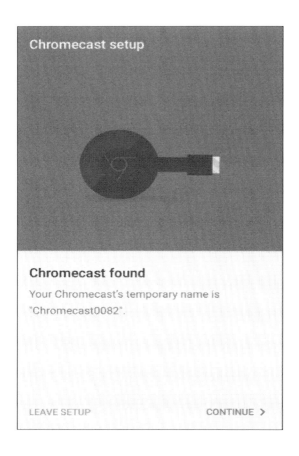

Next, the setup application will pillar an affirmation code to your TV—the people at Google are unmistakably intense about ensuring you're setting up the privilege Chromecast. Affirm that you see the code by tapping "I See It."

Next, you'll be incited to choose your area (e.g. Joined States). Snap "Proceed with." You'll be provoked to name your Chromecast. As a matter of course it has the haphazardly produced name (e.g. "Chromecast0089"), yet the best activity is name it by the room it's in (e.g. "Bedroom" or "Living Room") for usability.

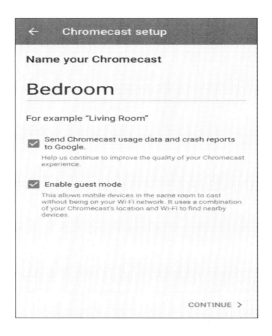

Notwithstanding naming it, you can likewise pick regardless of whether your Chromecast will send crash reports to Google and regardless of whether Guest Mode is empowered. The crash detailing bit is clear as crystal, yet in the event that you'd get a kick out of the chance to peruse more about Guest Mode (which enables visitors to utilize your Chromecast without signing into your Wi-Fi) Don't stress over irregular individuals associating with your Chromecast starting from the apartment the lobby; Guest Mode expects them to see the genuine screen and utilize the PIN on the screen keeping in mind the end goal to interface.

Once you've influenced your determination, to click "Proceed" and afterward connect to the certifications for the Wi-Fi organize you wish to associate the Chromecast to. On the off chance that you have various Wi-Fi organizes in your house, make sure to put the Chromecast on the Wi-Fi arrange you ordinarily use on your telephone or tablet, since that is the thing that you'll be throwing from.

In conclusion, you can (alternatively) interface your Google record to your Chromecast. While you don't have to do this, on the off chance that you wish to utilize a portion of the propelled highlights of the Chromecast (like modifying the settings with your own particular photographs), you do need to interface the Chromecast to your Google account.

Banner Tom

Sign in for a better Chromecast experience

Link your device to your Google account to personalize your experience when using Google products.

SKIP   SIGN IN ⟩

CHAPTER FIVE

HOW TO EASILY STREAM MUSIC AND VIDEO INTO YOUR CHROMECAST

There are two approaches to utilize the Chromecast. You can cast from a cell phone and you can cast from your PC from Chrome. In the event that you need the full once-over on the work area throwing choice, look at our manual for Chromecast reflecting here. In spite of the fact that the work area throwing capacity has its uses, the portable throwing knowledge is much more cleaned and absolutely the wellspring of the Chromecast's ubiquity.

To exploit Chromecast's simple throwing, you simply need to get an application that has throwing implicit, for example, YouTube, Netflix, or Pandora. Once you've stacked an application with Chromecast similarity, playback is as simple as can be (and this usability is unquestionably why the Chromecast is so fiercely famous).

Simply open a video and tap the Chromecast logo, seen underneath in the upper right-hand corner of the screen capture. The portable application you're utilizing will consequently kick the stream over to the Chromecast and the stream will start playback.

The additional pleasant thing about the Chromecast is that all the unloading/decompression of the video stream is taken care of by the Chromecast itself (not the throwing gadget), so regardless of whether your gadget is old, battered, and donning a moderate processor, you can in any case utilize the Chromecast effortlessly. A such, old Android and iOS gadgets make for incredible Chromecast "remote controls" you can leave connected to beside the sofa in the family room.

That is everything to setting up your Chromecast. When you have it introduced, you've jabbed around the application for a moment or two, and you have an idea about the exceptionally straightforward tap the-symbol throwing usefulness it's all smooth cruising.

THE END

Made in the USA
Las Vegas, NV
26 December 2024

15344880R00015